The Old Woman
who lived in a
Vinegar Bottle

The Old Woman who lived in a Vinegar Bottle

RUMER GODDEN

Illustrated by

MAIRI HEDDERWICK

M

MACMILLAN CHILDREN'S BOOKS

Another Picturemac by Rumer Godden
with illustrations by Lynne Byrnes

A KINDLE OF KITTENS

ISBN 0333 32965 1

First published 1972
Reprinted 1973, 1979 by
MACMILLAN LONDON LIMITED
London and Basingstoke

Associated companies in Auckland, Delhi, Dublin,
Gabarone, Hamburg, Harare, Hong Kong, Johannesburg,
Kuala Lumpur, Lagos, Manzini, Melbourne, Mexico City,
Nairobi, New York, Singapore and Tokyo

Picturemac edition published 1982
Reprinted 1983, 1985, 1986

Printed in Spain

This is an old folk tale that has had different names and different versions. I do not know where this one originally came from except that it used to be told to my mother by her nurse on hair-washing nights. My mother told it to me; I told it to my children and now they tell it to their children—on hair-washing nights—so that in our family alone it is four generations old.

Why it was, and is, told on hair-washing occasions I do not know either but the two went so well together that the story is always connected in my mind with the warmth of the fire seen through tangles of wet hair, the smell of damp towels and the fresh scent of shampoo.

As far as I know this is the first time this version has been written down—but I must take the responsibility of adding Malt.

R.G.

Once upon a time there was an old woman who lived in a vinegar bottle.★

★ It was probably an old oast house of the kind used for drying hops, half a kiln and half a tower, but it must have been built too small and lost its wind vane—or never had one. Someone had painted its walls stone grey and given its pointed roof a thatch instead of tiles. The villagers called it 'the vinegar bottle' because vinegar used to be made in thick stone bottles with glazed yellow necks.

There was a round room downstairs and a round room up, but that was smaller and had a pointed roof; the windows were small and the front door narrow—it was the only door. The corkscrew staircase came up in the middle of the bedroom floor. The vinegar bottle was not exactly comfortable but the old woman did not mind. "There's no place like home," said the old woman.

In the sitting room downstairs she had a table and chair and a dresser set out with her bits of china. She had made a rag rug to go in front of the fire, and by it was her high-backed wooden rocking chair. Upstairs, for her bed she had made a patchwork quilt "from pieces of all the dresses I have ever had since I was seven." A wooden box that stood upright made a place to put her candlestick, and there were some useful pegs on which to hang her clothes.

Outside, on the bottle wall, a tin bath hung from a nail—the old woman had a bath every Saturday night; there was a pail for carrying water, a dustpan and a broom, and a small black kettle that sang to itself on the hob all day long. "What more can a body want?" asked the old woman.

The vinegar bottle stood by itself on the edge of a wide lake, with a path that led to the shore; the old woman had edged the path with shells.

Though she was poor, she was most particular and kept the vinegar bottle tidy and specklessly clean; the door-step was whitened, the windows shone and there was always a pencil of smoke coming up from the chimney—"I like a good fire," said the old woman. She spent a deal of her time picking up sticks and driftwood from the lake shore or cutting turves for her peat stack. There was no one to help her because she lived quite alone. "Alone? Not a bit of it. Haven't I Malt?" said the old woman.

Malt was her cat.

The old woman did not have much to eat. Every Monday she went to the village and bought a screw of tea, three ounces of sugar and a pound bag of flour. When she got home she baked two loaves. "They last the week," she said. When the butcher's van came round, she bought "pieces and trimmings", left-over meat; she cooked them for Malt but kept the dripping to spread on her toast. On Tuesdays and Fridays she walked to the farm and had her pannikin filled with milk—most of that went to Malt as well. Now and again the farmer's wife gave her a couple of eggs and the farmer let her pick up the potatoes left in the field—the old woman called them "taters". In autumn she picked blackberries and made blackberry jelly with the sugar she had saved and often she found windfall apples in the grass. "A little more *would* be good," said the old woman. "But taking it all in all, it's enough for the likes of me."

Malt was twice as fat as the old woman.

One Saturday morning in early summer, the old woman was hungry; whether she had cut the slices thicker, or the loaf was smaller she did not know, but there were only two crusts left to last until Monday. Her blackberry jelly was finished, it was not the season for apples; she must keep the milk for Malt—"except a drop for my tea"— and there was just a handful of potatoes. "One for dinner, one for supper. You must make do with that," she told herself and went about her work as cheerfully as she could. When the village clock struck noon she made up the fire, swept the hearth with a turkey wing she kept for that purpose, put on a clean apron and sat down in her rocking chair because she felt a little weak.

The rocking chair was hard but it rested her old bones. It had once had a red cushion, but Malt found the cushion comfortable and it was now on the other side of the hearth with Malt curled up on it, his paws tucked in and his eyes shut as he purred.

As it was such a fine morning, the old woman had left the door ajar so that, as she sat, she could look across the lake where a fishing boat was coming in; she watched it as she rocked. It was peaceable by the fire. Rock:purr:purr:rock. Then she stopped rocking. "Dust!" said the old woman. "Dust on my clean floor."

Malt opened an eye but did not stir.

The sun, shining on the clean stone flags, showed a sprinkling of dust where the wind had blown in from the path; it was only a sprinkling but the old woman fetched her broom and began to sweep, sweeping every speck towards the door. The fishing boat was coming in to land. Suddenly the old woman stopped again. Something in the dust was glinting silver in the sun, something small and round

A button? The old woman bent and picked it up. It was not a button but a silver sixpence. "Lordy! Well, I never did!" said the old woman.

Malt opened the other eye.

Sixpence! A whole silver sixpence! The old woman was so excited she forgot to put away her broom but stood in the doorway looking at the sixpence in her hand.

The fishermen had grounded their boat and were unloading their net and rods and a big bucket that seemed heavy. "Full o' fish," said the old woman, and then, "I know what I'll do. I'll buy me a fish for my dinner. It's years and years since I had a bit of fish. Fish and a 'tater. What a feast!"

As soon as he heard the word "fish" Malt jumped up. He had not tasted it for a long time, either. He decided to accompany the old woman down to the shore.

"Can't buy much of a fish for that," said the fisherman when the old woman offered her sixpence. "Fish is very very scarce."

"And very very dear."

"Oh well. You can have this little 'un," and one of the men took the money and tossed a small fish into the old woman's hand.

Malt tried to stand on his hind legs to look.

The little fish lay in the old woman's hand; it was still alive, its mouth opening and shutting while its tail twitched.

"'Tis small for certain," said the old woman. "Still, the middle'll be enough for me, the head and tail for Malt." Malt set up a miaowing and rubbed himself against her skirt. He was hungry too.

The fish gasped in the hurtful air. Its gills lifted up and down; they were lined with scarlet while the rest of it was silver; its eyes seemed to be looking at the lake.

"I'll cook it in milk with herbs." The old woman said it slowly as she looked at the dying little fish. "Eat it with 'taters."

The fish's gills pumped up and down as it gasped; its tail gave a helpless twitch.

"With 'taters," but the old woman knew she could not bear it any more. She ran to the water's edge and threw the little fish plop back into the lake.

Malt gave a miaoul of anguish and the fishermen stared.

"Whatever did you do that for?"

"Gone and thrown away your dinner."

"I know," said the old woman.

"Daft," and one of the fishermen tapped his forehead.

"Off her crumpet," said the other one and laughed. They picked up their gear and their catch and set off to the village still laughing.

Malt stalked away to sulk behind the peat stack.

The old woman was left alone on the lake shore. She felt old and
silly—and hungry.

She had turned to go back to her vinegar bottle when a sound made
her stop. There were ripples in the lake; then the water went bubble
bubble bubble and up came the little fish.

"Old woman . . ."

Now it was the old woman who gasped; her knees nearly gave way and for a moment the lake shore seemed to turn round and round, but the little fish spoke quite calmly.

"Old woman."

"Yes—sir." She did not know if one can call a fish "sir" but then she had not known that anywhere in the world there was a fish that talked.

"You are a dear kind old woman, and as unselfish as you are kind."

"Thank you . . . sir."

"You should say 'sire' not 'sir'," said the fish. "Or Highness. You may not know it but I am the ruler of this lake. I look like a fish but I am a prince."

"Lordy! Lordy!" said the old woman.

"Not a lord, a prince," and now she thought she could see a band of gold around his head—or was it that she was dazzled by the light? "But no matter," said the fish. "You saved my life so you may call me 'little fish'; and good old woman, anything you want, I shall grant."

"Thank you kindly, sir, prince, Highness," stammered the old woman. "Thank you, I'm sure, but I don't want anything."

"Well if you do, you have only to come to the lake shore and call, 'Little fish, little fish,' and I shall come," and the fish sank back into the water leaving only rings of ripples where it had been.

The old woman made a deep curtsey.

Back in the vinegar bottle the old woman had to sit down plump in her chair; her knees had really given way and she felt all of a shiver and shake. A fish that talked! A fish who was a prince! "Must have been dreaming. It couldn't be." But it was. There was a smell of fish on her hand and one tiny silver fish scale. "It was," she said over and over again as she rocked. "It was." Then her glance fell on Malt's empty cushion. She stopped rocking and sat quite still.

"Of all the silly old bodies!" she said. "The men were right. I'm daft. I was that flabbergasted, I suppose." She stood up and looked towards the lake, half afraid. "Go on, you silly old goose," the old woman told herself. Next minute she was standing on the lake shore.

"Little fish. Little fish." Her voice was shaking so much, it sounded like 'Li^{tt}le f^{is}h' but the water went bubble bubble bubble and up came the little fish.

The old woman curtsied. "Excuse me for bothering you, I'm sure but . . . but, there is one thing I very much need." She was twisting her apron into a knot. "You see there's but two crusts left and hardly any 'taters and I must keep the milk and meat for Malt—that's my cat— so . . . Oh, little fish, sir, Highness, do you think you could give us— Malt and me—a good hot dinner?"

"Go home and you will find one," said the little fish.

When the old woman reached home, what a sight met her eyes— and what a smell! Malt had smelt it too and had come running from the peat-stack.

Her table was covered with a damask cloth and set with plates, dishes, silver and glass. She stole closer to look. There was a covered bowl of soup, a plate of hot roast beef "with Yorkshire pudding, roast 'taters, greens and gravy," she whispered. There was an apple tart for one, with fresh cream: two bread rolls keeping warm in a white napkin: a little pat of butter: a little wedge of cheese and a small brown jug of ale. On the floor by Malt's cushion was a bowl of meat, a saucer of milk and a catnip mouse.

"Lordy! Lordy! Lordy!" said the old woman. "Glory be!"

Malt was already gobbling but, before she touched a morsel, the old woman felt she had to go back to the lake and say 'thank you'. She did

not call "Little fish" but simply called "Thank you kindly," across the lake and curtsied again.

Never in all their lives had she and Malt tasted such a dinner—and the old woman did not even have to wash it up.

After they had eaten, they felt too comfortable to move and fell asleep, one each side of the fire. When they woke up the table was cleared and there was a note in rippling writing, *Another one tomorrow*.

A storm blew up on the lake that night. The vinegar bottle was sturdy and the old woman had slept through a hundred such storms, but that night she lay awake listening to the wind and rain—perhaps she had eaten too much dinner. The roof will blow off, she thought; the wind will lift the thatch, and, when the wind buffeted the walls, "Lord, we shall blow right over," she said. Malt was not worried; he was sound asleep under the patchwork quilt at the foot of the bed but the old woman lay and quaked. Suddenly she sat up. "Lordy!" she said aloud. "Why didn't I think of that afore?"

She would have gone down to the lake as soon as it was daylight but thought it polite to wait until the little fish had finished his breakfast—if fishes have breakfast—but it was still early when she stood at the water's edge and called.

"Little fish. Little fish."

The water went bubble bubble bubble and up came the little fish.

"If you please," and the old woman curtsied. "If you please, little fish, I'm that tired of living in the vinegar bottle. It's not at all comfortable and I'm getting elderly. Would it be too much trouble to let me have a cottage—a very little cottage?" pleaded the old woman, "but if it had proper rooms and I didn't have to carry water . . . a bit of garden perhaps, perhaps a garden gate—if it's not any trouble. If there was a rose or two . . . a little cottage."

"Go home and you will find one," said the little fish.

She turned round; then she rubbed her eyes because she could not believe what she saw. "Eh! I didn't know it would be *that* quick!"

Where the vinegar bottle had been was a cottage with white walls and a pretty tiled roof. The windows had leaded panes and were hung with muslin curtains. There was a front door with a brass knocker and red roses climbing the walls.

Half afraid, the old woman opened the gate—there was a wicket gate—and saw a patch of garden, small but filled with flowers. "Pansies, lilies, pinks, all sorts. It can't be mine, it can't," whispered the old woman, but, though the gate now came across the path, there were her own shells on the path edges and there was Malt coming down it to meet her. Malt did not know if he were on his head or his paws.

When she opened the door into a sitting room, her rocking chair was one side of the fire, Malt's cushion on the other, the rag rug between them. In the little dining-room were her table and chair, the dresser with her bits of china. In the kitchen the black kettle was singing on a new stove; the broom and dustpan set in a corner. The tin bath had disappeared; it was no longer needed; upstairs was a bathroom that had—"Hot water"! whispered the old woman. Her hand shook as she turned on the taps—she had never had a tap before. Next door was a bedroom, a proper bedroom for her bed, the box for the candlestick, her useful pegs. There was a little spare bedroom in the attic.

"Lordy! Lordy! Lordy!" said the old woman and when she came downstairs she was shaking so much that again she had to sit down. Malt sat with his tail round his paws and made noises under his breath as if he were saying, "Where is my vinegar bottle?"

The sun came in at the door, bringing the scent of roses and the old woman had tears in her eyes. "God bless the little fish." Presently she went through the rooms again, came and sat down, went through them again. The tears had dried and, "Looks terrible bare," said the old woman.

Her things, that had suited the vinegar bottle, looked battered and mean in the cottage. "Even the rocker's terrible old and the rug's that faded." In a cottage like this a candlestick should not be kept on a box, clothes hung on pegs. "A cupboard, a new bed," said the old woman, "and down here a grandfather clock"—she had never needed a clock; she listened for the church clock chimes—"A sofy; chairs for visitors"— she had never had a visitor. "Malt should have a basket"—he had never had a basket—"Wonder if I durst ask?" said the old woman. "No, I

dursn't," but in a few moments she was calling, "Little fish. Little fish."

The water went bubble bubble bubble and up came the little fish.

"The cottage is so pretty, the roses and all. I don't know how to thank you, but . . ." The little fish was just disappearing in his rings of ripples, when he heard the 'but' and stopped.

"I ought to have mentioned it afore." The old woman was apologetic, "but I meant a furnished cottage. My old furniture isn't fitting—so please, *dear* little fish . . ."

"Go home and you will find some," said the little fish.

A grandfather clock was ticking against the wall: there was a blue sofa and two blue chairs: the rag rug had gone; in its place lay a carpet scattered with roses, "To match the ones outside," whispered the old woman. A basket with a blue cushion was ready for Malt and an elegant table stood in the window. The dining room was elegant too with new chairs and a mahogany table. "Soon it will be set with a good hot dinner. Was there ever such a lucky old woman as I?" The kitchen had shining new pans, the kettle was new; fresh geraniums flowered in pots on the sill. Upstairs was a four poster bed with blue and white chintz curtains: the box was gone and the candlestick; there was a table with a shaded light, "and a real dressing table and stool and a cupboard," marvelled the old woman. In the cupboard her "other" dress hung—she had only two. As the cupboard door swung open it had a long mirror and, for the first time in her life, the old woman saw herself from head to toe. "Lordy," said the old woman. "Is that really I?"

She stared at herself, stated and stared. Her clothes, that had looked quite right in the vinegar bottle, seemed "Terrible shabby. You're a proper old ragbag," the old woman told the old woman in the mirror.

She came downstairs and sat in one of the new blue chairs by the fire. She tried to rock but of course it was not a rocking chair. Malt would not go in his new basket; he sat on the rug and fixed the old woman with his eyes. He was plainly asking, "Where is my cushion?" but she took no notice. "Proper old rag-bag," said the old woman slowly.

Then she got up and went down to the lake.

"Little fish. Little fish."

The water went bubble bubble bubble and up came the little fish.

"A rag-bag, that's what I look," the old woman had to burst it out almost before the fish had his head out of the water. "A proper old rag-bag. I can't live in that lovely cottage with its lovely furniture, dressed like this. Little fish, little fish, I must, I must have some new clothes."

The little fish said, "Look."

At first the old woman did not know where to look. She looked behind her, on each side and up at the sky. Then she looked down and, "Lordy!" she said.

She was wearing a new blue dress sprigged with flowers and a new pink apron. On her feet were buckled shoes and she had warm white stockings; as she bent to gaze at them—those shining buckles—she caught a glimpse of a scarlet petticoat. Nor was that all. When she got back to the cottage, she found other clothes in the cupboards—dresses were hanging up. "Mercy me! I'll never wear all those," said the old woman. A warm red cloak with a hood hung on a peg, with a beautiful new shawl. Folded on shelves were underclothes, nightgowns, more stockings; there was even a pile of handkerchiefs scented with lavender. "Nothing forgotten or amiss," whispered the old woman.

Malt came and sniffed her and his whiskers went stiff. "You don't look like my old woman. You don't smell like my old woman," he seemed to say. He edged away and would not rub himself against her skirts.

How careful the old woman was when she ate her dinner that day; as the note had promised, it appeared on the table at noon: tomato soup and sausages—"I had forgotten how tasty they are." For "afters" as she called them, there was ice cream. "Can't remember when I last tasted that." It was all so good but not a drop nor a spot must be spilt on her new dress, and she scolded Malt and boxed his ears when his whiskers dribbled milk on the floor. "I can't help my whiskers. They always dribble," Malt might have said, but the old woman scolded, "Drat the cat! I'll have to wipe the milk up and might dirty my new apron." That brought a thought: the cottage must be cleaned—the old woman never let a day pass without cleaning—"And a cottage takes a deal more keeping than a vinegar bottle," said the old woman. "Carry out the ashes from the fire, bring in peat and wood, dust, sweep, polish, scrub. How can I *scrub* in my new clothes? T'would be a sin and a shame," the old woman said to Malt. Malt did not answer. He was sulking but again she did not notice. She had made up her mind and the next moment was hurrying down to the lake.

"Little fish. Little fish."

He looked as if he might say, "You again!" but before he could speak the old woman had begun. "You couldn't really expect it." She sounded out of temper and the fish's fins rose in surprise. "Expect me to do housework in these fine new clothes. As I said to Malt, t'would be a sin and a shame. You ought to have thought of it yourself, little fish. You said I should have everything I want. Well, I want a maid."

"Go home and you will find one," said the little fish. His voice was quiet after the old woman's, quiet—and a shade tired.

The maid's name was Amelia; in a cap and apron and a neat black dress she was waiting at the cottage door when the old woman came up from the lake. "Would you like a cup of tea, Ma'am?"

No one had called the old woman "Ma'am" before and she was so flustered that she said, "Yes," though she had only just finished her dinner—too much dinner, thought the old woman. She had indigestion.

After her tea she could not settle down in the blue chair; for one thing it would not rock—"and I am used to the rocking"—for another Amelia was busy about the house and, "We're used to being alone, Malt and me," thought the old woman. Malt could not settle either. Where was their peaceable rock :purr :purr :rock? Amelia came in and out with her duster and her questions. "She fidgets me," and the old woman went upstairs. She decided to change her clothes. "Well, I have nothing else to do."

She had put on a grey silk dress with a rustling white petticoat when, through the open window, she heard the sound of bells. "If 'tisn't Sunday! That's for afternoon service," and she thought she would go to church and show off her new clothes to the village.

"I am going to church, Amelia."

"Yes, Ma'am," said Amelia.

"Take care of Malt. I shall soon be back."

"Yes, Ma'am." Then Amelia said, "You're never going to walk there in those shoes." The old woman had been going to walk, she always walked to the village but the buckled shoes were thin compared to her old clogs, and they pinched her corns compared to her old slippers. "Are you going to *walk?*"

"No, indeed," said the old woman and marched down to the lake.

"Little fish. Little fish."

The water went bubble bubble bubble and up came the little fish.

"I have a maid now, little fish, and can leave the house when I choose. With these new clothes it's a waste to stay at home so I am going to church." The old woman did not know it but she spoke in a hoity-toity voice. The fish said nothing but looked at the old woman a little sadly. "Kindly order me a conveyance"—she did not know herself how she found such a grand word—"a conveyance, my good fish."

"Go home and you will find one," said the patient little fish.

A tub cart and pony stood at the cottage gate. The tub cart was smart, dark green with scarlet wheels; there was a whip in a wicker holder, a red and green checked rug to put over the old woman's knees, and the reins and harness were scarlet. The pony was dapple grey. Amelia was stroking its mane and giving it lumps of sugar. "Oh Ma'am, isn't it the prettiest little pony in the whole wide world?" said Amelia. It was, but the old woman did not seem to think so; she looked at it, sniffed in disdain and turned straight back to the lake.

"Little fish. Little fish."

The water went bubble bubble bubble and up came the little fish.

"You didn't understand." The old woman sounded almost as if she were scolding. "When I said a conveyance, of course I meant a car. "Who," she asked with scorn, "Who goes about in a pony and cart these days? Of course I meant a car."

"Go home and you will find one," said the little fish, and he went back into the water with a sharp flop.

The pony and trap had gone; in their place was a small red car, its seats covered in good black leather; it had a red steering wheel and seemed just right for an old woman to drive but, "That stupid fish!" cried the old woman. "I didn't mean a car like *that*." and again she turned straight back to the lake.

"Little fish. Little fish." She stamped her foot.

The water went bubble bubble bubble and up came the little fish.

"You are making fun of me," said the furious old woman. "What can I do with a niminy car like that? You know quite well that I can't drive. I meant, of course a car with a chauffeur, a great big shining car like the Queen's. How else, in my silk dress, can I go to church? A car with a chauffeur *if* you please, and at once or I'll be late."

The little fish did not say, "Go home and you will find one," but stood up out of the water on his silver tail. "You used to curtsey to me," said the little fish. "Yesterday you came and said 'thank you' before you touched a morsel of the dinner I sent you. That was yesterday, only yesterday, but now! You are a greedy ungrateful old woman," said the little fish. "Go back to your vinegar bottle."

And before the first ripple had spread its ring, the grey silk dress was gone, and the old woman was back in her shabby old dress, her faded print apron and slippers. The cottage, the furniture, the clothes, Amelia and the car had vanished; back in its old place was the vinegar bottle.

Malt was miaowing on the path, his fur on end. Then he ran purring towards his old home.

It was a miserable old woman who crept down to the lake that evening; she stood on the shore and called, "Little fish. Little fish."

She did not think he would come but presently the water went bubble bubble bubble and up came the little fish.

"What do you want?"

"To say I'm sorry." The old woman wiped her eyes on the corner of her apron. "Forgive me for troubling you but I'm that sorry and ashamed—not sorry because of the cottage and the other beautiful things—sorry to have been so rude and so ungrateful. You're quite right, little fish. I'm a greedy grabbing old woman and I didn't know it. I don't know what got into me and that's the truth. I'm sorry and please forgive me, and thank you kindly, and goodbye, little fish."

She curtsied and turned to go but the little fish called, "Old woman."

"Old woman, I'm glad," said the little fish. "I thought this was to be a sad story and it isn't at all. You are still the generous kind old woman I thought you. And now I shall make the cottage and furniture, your clothes and the maid, and the pony and cart or the car—which you like—come back and you shall have them for always," but the old woman shook her head.

"Thank you kindly, little fish, but no. Malt and me, we're best in our vinegar bottle. We're used to it, you see. I missed my rocker and Malt missed his cushion, and I like to be busy and fend for myself. Thank you kindly but we'll stay as we are, except . . ." she stopped.

"Except?" asked the little fish gently.

"If 'twouldn't be greedy, do you think, now and then, sir, sire, prince, Highness, you could send us a good hot dinner? Not too often of course, and please don't clear it away. Why, one of those dinners would keep Malt and me for a week. I'll wash it up," said the old woman.

The old woman still lives in the vinegar bottle.

As she sits rocking, she often thinks of the little fish who talked and wore a golden circle on his silver head. She knows he was not a dream because every Sunday, as the village church clock strikes noon, a hot dinner appears on her table, another by the cushion for Malt.

Malt is now three times as fat as the old woman.